MW01257944

The
Wizard Owl

—— Idella Bodie

SANDLAPPER PUBLISHING CO., INC.

ORANGEBURG, SOUTH CAROLINA 29115

© 2003 by Idella Bodie

All rights reserved.

Second Printing, 2007

Published by Sandlapper Publishing Co., Inc.
          Orangeburg, South Carolina 29115

Manufactured in the United States of America
by McNaughton & Gunn, Inc.

Library of Congress Cataloging-in-Publication Data

Bodie, Idella.
    The wizard owl / Idella Bodie.—1st ed.
        p. cm. — (Heroes and heroines of the American Revolution)
    ISBN 0-87844-167-0 (pbk.)
    Summary: A biography of General Andrew Pickens, which
describes his role in the Indian wars, the Revolutionary War, and as
a representative from South Carolina to the United States Congress.
    Includes bibliographical references.
    1. Pickens, Andrew, 1739–1817—Juvenile literature. 2. Gener-
als—United States—Biography—Juvenile literature. 3. South
Carolina—History—Revolution, 1775–1783—Juvenile literature. 4.
South Carolina—Militia—Biography—Juvenile literature. [1.
Pickens, Andrew, 1739–1817. 2. Generals. 3. Legislators. 4. South
Carolina—History—Revolution, 1775–1783.] I. Title.

E207.P63 B63 2003
975.7'03'09B—dc21

                                                    2003002666

Acknowledgement

I am indebted to Alice Noble Waring
for her biography of Andrew Pickens,
The Fighting Elder.

ANDREW PICKENS was one of the foremost figures of the American Revolution in South Carolina, North Carolina, and Georgia.

To the Young Reader

Andrew Pickens is not as well known as Thomas Sumter and Francis Marion for his part in the Revolutionary War. However, he did for the Up Country of South Carolina what these other heroes did for the Low Country.

Andrew grew up in South Carolina with the Cherokee Indians as neighbors. He formed a close bond with the Indians and learned their culture. He loved the land they loved. As an adult, he settled near them in the Long Canes area, present-day Abbeville County.

When the time came that frontier settlers in the Up Country had to fight the Indians or move to other areas, Congress chose Pickens to lead that fight. He found his duty to go to war against his Indian friends very painful. Yet he felt he had no choice. The killings of entire white families must be stopped.

Pickens often defeated the Indians using skills he learned from them. Because of this, they both honored and feared him. The Cherokees called him Skyagunsta, the Indian word for "Wizard Owl."

As an officer in the Revolutionary War, Pickens gained fame in the Battle of Cowpens. The Up Country volunteers, who made up most of his militia, knew the land well. They hunted it to feed their families. This knowledge made them good scouts in locating the enemy. Throughout the war, Pickens's militia respected and followed him wherever he served.

History remembers Pickens chiefly for his peacemaking efforts with the Indians before, during, and after the Revolutionary War.

Contents

1.
Early Years

No one knows what Andrew Pickens was like as a boy. Judging from his adult personality, he must have been shy. Records show him as a quiet man who rarely smiled. If anyone ever heard him laugh, the event was not recorded.

Andrew was born in Paxtang, Pennsylvania, on September 19, 1739. He was still a baby when his family joined others on the Great Wagon Trail to the Shenandoah Valley in Virginia.

At thirteen, Andrew moved with his parents to the Waxhaws settlement of South Carolina to live with other Scotch Irish. Waxhaw Indians, who once lived on the land, had joined the Catawbas on the west side of the Catawba River.

Cane fields and forests covered the rolling land. Boulders of granite stood here and there, but the ground was good for growing crops and grazing cattle. An Indian trading path crossed the land.

The Pickenses were loyal members of Waxhaws Presbyterian Church. Long sermons often held them for hours in the meeting house. Quiet by nature, Andrew was probably a good listener.

Since settlers never knew when Indians might attack, the men took their rifles to church. A guard kept watch outside.

Although songs and prayers filled much of life in the Waxhaws, the citizens had their share of quarrels. Andrew's father settled many of these arguments. Andrew enjoyed listening to the cases in court. He later said it was his father's fairness in these cases that taught him respect for the law.

When Andrew was sixteen, the death of his father ended his hope for higher education.

2.
Frontier Country

Settlers in the Up Country of South Carolina lived close to one of the most powerful Indian nations in the country: the Cherokee. At first the Cherokees made friends with the settlers. They even signed a peace treaty with the British who ruled the colonists.

During his teen years Andrew learned the ways of the Indians. He knew they loved the songs of birds and the cries of wild animals breaking the silence of the forests.

As settlers moved in, instead of sounds of nature, the crack of gunfire and the sawing of trees broke the silence.

Settlers came in large numbers and built new homes. They cleared land for crops and hunted the forests for game. Deer became so scarce, the Indians said, they could hardly feed or clothe their families.

Andrew understood the Indians' feelings. The sense of justice he learned in his father's court made him question what was happening. Was it right for the settlers to take land the Indians had lived on for generations?

Though some Cherokees remained friendly, others attacked white settlements. They burned homes and scalped and murdered settlers. The British, they said, had broken their treaties.

Fear of attack caused some frontier families to build stockades around their homes. Others moved to safer places near the coast.

The Calhoun family was among those who

joined a wagon train headed west. Along the way
their wagons mired in a swamp near Long Cane
Creek and Indians swooped down upon them.

During the massacre, a blue-eyed, black-
haired girl of fourteen, Becky Calhoun, crouched
unnoticed in a canebrake. When Becky's uncle
returned later to gather the dead for burial, he
found her. All of her family had been killed. He
took her to live with relatives in the Waxhaws
area.

Andrew and Becky met when he was seventeen years old. Shy Andrew fell under the spell of Miss Rebecca's beauty. Before a romance had time to blossom, Andrew left home to fight against the Cherokees.

He became captain of volunteers from the Waxhaws area. Although he was the youngest man in his company, he soon gained the respect of the others.

Both the Indians and the whites had broken promises and behaved cruelly. A full-fledged war soon began.

Andrew found it hard to fight against Indians he had known since he was a boy. Even years later, as an old man, he could not forget the killings and the burning of villages. "It was there," he said, "I learned how cruel war is."

3.
Family Man

When the Cherokee War ended, Pickens returned home. His mother had died, his sisters were married, and his brothers no longer needed him on the farm. Becky had been on his mind thoughout the war. He hurried to ask her to marry him and she accepted.

After a big wedding, Pickens took his bride to live in the Long Canes area, near the present-day city of Abbeville. He chose a site for their home near a spring. The Pickens homesite was a favorite spot for travelers. Becky made friends with the people who camped under their trees. Always in high spirits, she brightened the travelers' way.

Pickens farmed and served as justice of the peace, as his father had done. He also carried on the Presbyterian faith of his youth, holding church services under a big chestnut tree near their house. He arranged to have visiting ministers give the sermons.

Standing almost six feet tall and slender, Pickens had a stern, stiff look. He tied his hair back from his long, lean face in a queue and often wore a three-cornered hat. Heavy spurs wrapped his boot heels and two large pistols hung at his waist.

Although times were peaceful, Pickens and others still feared an Indian uprising. As a precaution, Pickens built a blockhouse near their home. It was actually a fort with a foundation of stone and walls of thick logs. A stream of water, diverted from the spring, ran in a tunnel under the fort. When occupants needed water, they lifted a stone in the floor.

In peacetime the blockhouse served as a trading post. Indians brought herbs gathered from the woods and skins of beavers and deer. They traded these for farm tools, cooking utensils, handmade cloth, and other goods.

For a while life was pleasant. Then something happened.

4.
The Revolutionary War

Unrest in the colonies led to a revolt against Mother England. In South Carolina news came that 3,000 Cherokees would join the British and Tories against the Patriots.

As a Patriot, Captain Andrew Pickens recruited companies of men to fight. Since he knew the Cherokees and their land, Congress asked him to scout out the Cherokee situation.

Twenty-five men joined Pickens. These volunteers wore deerskin trousers and rough woolen shirts made by their wives and daughters, raccoon skin caps, and homemade leather moccasins. Since they had no uniforms, each wore a green twig to show he was Patriot.

Many of the men carried rifles. Powder horns dangled from their shoulders and large hunting knives hung from their belts. Instead of swords, which they did not have, some carried scythes. A few had pitchforks.

About two miles into their trip, they came to an old Indian field covered with grass four or five feet high. As the scouts crossed the field, hundreds of Indian braves, painted for war, rose in a wide circle around them. With rifles swinging in one hand and tomahawks in the other, the braves rushed to surround Pickens and his militia.

Seeing such a small group, the chief commanded the braves to take scalps.

The warriors dropped their rifles, raised their tomahawks, and rushed forward.

"Turn to face them!" shouted Pickens.

His men did an about-face, forming a small ring inside the circle.

"Hold your fire until I shoot," Pickens ordered. "Then fire twice, fall into the grass, reload, rise, and fire again."

When the Indians came within twenty yards, Pickens fired. His men followed orders. Shots rang out. Two warriors fell.

Other warriors drew back, falling against each other. Some dropped their tomahawks, grabbed their rifles, and fired upon the Patriots.

The Patriot scouts fought for their lives. They fired, fell, and rose again. Now and then a warrior broke through the ring, and a bloody hand-to-hand battle followed.

At the worst of the fighting, Pickens's gun

failed to fire. He snatched up a wounded scout's gun and continued.

Finally, the remaining Indians withdrew.

The success of Pickens's "Ring Fight" and his courage during the battle amazed the Indians. They gave him the name Skyagunsta. In their language it meant Wizard Owl or Great Warrior.

5.
The Slave Savior

Unlike military men of today, volunteer soldiers of the Revolutionary War were free to go home to check on their families unless they were needed in a battle. Pickens divided his free time between recruiting volunteers and visiting with his family.

He built a heavy stockade around the blockhouse for his family's protection. He also built a powder magazine for storing ammunition on top of a nearby hill.

Friends and neighbors gathered at the blockhouse for safety. It became known as Fort Pickens.

When Pickens was on the battlefield, Tories often threatened his family. But Cherokee warriors believed the tall, slender man who rode among them without fear had some mysterious power. They made sure they did not come close to his home.

Sometimes when her husband was away, Becky moved into the blockhouse with her children and house servants. Once, awakened during the night by loud voices, she saw Tories outside their house. She rushed to wake the slaves and placed the sleeping children in their arms. Together, they slipped into the nearby woods.

Heavy summer rains left water standing in pools. The Pickenses' faithful slave, Dick, constructed a shelter from cane.

When morning came, Becky first checked on her children. Several had fever the night before. The dreaded disease smallpox spotted their little faces.

The baby died, and Becky said had it not been for their loyal slave all would have perished. With the Tories in their home, Dick sneaked to the blockhouse each night for food.

When it was safe for the family to return to the house, Dick led them home.

6.
A Man of Compassion

Pickens and his militia made many contributions to the war. Besides fighting the Cherokees, they fought at the Battle of Ninety Six.

After the Battle of Stono on the South Carolina coast, Pickens and his men protected General Lincoln's army in their retreat. During this time, a British soldier shot Pickens's horse from under him.

The militia under Pickens fought courageously in the Battle of Cowpens.

They also aided General Elijah Clarke in the siege of Augusta, Georgia, and later in the Battle of Kettle Creek while Clarke recovered from battle wounds and smallpox.

Along with many other Patriots, Pickens's militia fought in one of the last battles of the war, Eutaw Springs.

Although Andrew Pickens was a stern leader who demanded his men obey his orders, he was a man of compassion.

After the Battle of Kettle Creek, he allowed Tory prisoners to stay behind to gather their wounded and bury their dead. He instructed them to report to him afterwards and he would allow them to visit their families.

Before Pickens left the battlefield, he went to General Boyd, a wounded Tory he knew personally.

"Boyd," he said, "I am pained to see you suffering—and for such a cause."

Boyd raised up on one arm. "I glory in the cause, Sir," he said. "I'm dying for my King and country." Then he took a watch from his pocket, handed it to Pickens, and asked him to see that his wife got it.

Pickens stationed two of his men with Boyd, who was near death, to offer him water.

For a while after the Battle of Kettle Creek, the colony was at peace.

7.
Paroled

In 1778 the British decided they could end the war in a short time by invading the southern states. With the help of Indians and Tories, they traveled by land and sea to Charles Town, the capital city of South Carolina at that time.

While Indians and Tories in the Up Country plundered and burned homes and carried off slaves, a large British fleet sailed into Charles Town Harbor. The ships opened fire on the city.

The Patriots became trapped between the Ashley

and Cooper Rivers. They had no way of getting food and supplies. Still, they fought bravely on.

Smallpox ravaged the city, houses burned, and cannon fire killed women and children.

Finally, the Patriots had to surrender. General Benjamin Lincoln surrendered not only his own men and the city of Charles Town, but all troops and citizens in South Carolina. In his opinion it was useless to fight any longer.

Continental soldiers became prisoners. The British commander offered Pickens and other militiamen a choice. They could accept imprisonment or sign a promise, "giving one's parole." By signing, the men promised never to bear arms against the British again. In return, the families and homes of those Patriots would be protected.

Any person who broke the promise would be

treated as a traitor and hanged. Most Patriots felt the war was over. Pickens and his men lay down their rifles and headed home, but the general did not sign the parole promise.

On his journey, Tories stopped Pickens to question him. Discovering he had no signed parole paper, they took him prisoner. British colonel John Cruger remembered Pickens's leadership during the Battle of Star Fort at Ninety Six. He sent a letter to British Lord Cornwallis:

> *If you can get Pickens of Long Canes settlement to accept a command in the British army, then I believe every man in the country would declare allegiance to the King of England.*

Lord Cornwallis took Cruger's advice and contacted Pickens. The Patriot refused to accept the offer. He remained a prisoner.

In prison, Pickens worried about his family. Finally, seeing no other way to return home, he signed the parole promise. He agreed not to bear arms against the British in return for protection of his home and family.

8.
Back at Home

Like other pioneer women, Becky had a hard time without her husband. She did her best to manage the plantation. Slaves planted and harvested the crops and tended the cattle. Twelve-year-old Ezekiel got up early each day to oversee the work. Mary, the oldest daughter, cared for the younger children.

Weary from her responsibilities, Becky welcomed her husband back to their plantation at Long Canes. She now turned her attention to their children and the preserving of fruit and vegetables for winter, as well as the spinning of cotton for their clothing.

Pickens took charge of the farming and began raising saddle horses. He also hired a teacher for his children's home schooling and Ezekiel's preparation for college.

Almost all of the Pickenses' neighbors in the Up Country were Tories. Pickens worried over the unfair treatment of other Patriots living in the area. But he was a man of his word.

"I pledged my honor," he said. "I am bound by oath not to take up arms against the British or the Tories who fought on their side. Not until the British break the oath I signed will I rejoin the fight."

Knowing Pickens was still loyal to the Patriot cause, a Tory neighbor made sure the general heard about each British victory.

One day, as Pickens sat under a large oak in his yard polishing his silver-handled pistols, his children playing around him, a neighbor appeared. Pickens nodded his head to acknowledge the man's presence and kept on polishing.

For a while neither spoke. Then the visitor said, "It's no use for the rebels to keep on fighting the King. They're all going to be killed."

Without saying a word, Pickens stood up, took the neighbor by the arm, and led him to the gate. Then he stepped back and gave the Tory a resounding kick in the pants.

Shocked over such an outburst from a usually patient man, the fellow ran down the hill to his home without looking back.

9.
Broken Promises

Tories and British Lord Cornwallis's Redcoats continued to plunder South Carolina and Georgia and burn Patriots' homes. Soldiers and their families also feared Banastre Tarleton's cruelty.

Although it looked as if South Carolina and Georgia were lost to British control, some Patriots kept up the fight. Bands of militia under Thomas Sumter and Francis Marion still harassed the enemy.

To everyone's surprise, the Patriots were victorious in the Battle of King's Mountain.

Captain James McCall, who fought with

Pickens in other battles, rode to Long Canes to see his friend. He begged Pickens to rejoin the war. Thomas Sumter and Elijah Clarke also urged the general to fight.

Pickens could not, in good conscience, break his promise.

Not long after the visit from Captain McCall,

Tory and British soldiers swept through the Up Country in the worst destruction of the war. They burned houses and churches, throwing Bibles into the flames. They carried away slaves, shot cattle and sheep, and put settlers to death.

Then one day while Pickens was away, Becky and their children shivered outside in the cold while their home, outbuildings, and crops burned. The family still huddled in fear when Pickens returned.

Pickens comforted his family and got them settled into the blockhouse. Then he mounted his horse and rode to a British camp nearby. He reported the burning and the insult to his wife and children.

"You have broken your promise," he told a British officer. "Since you harmed my family and burned my home, I consider myself no longer bound by the oath I took."

The British commander respected Pickens. He knew the general as a man of his word. He begged him to change his mind.

Pickens refused and turned to leave. The officer made no effort to stop him but said, "We are at war against each other. I hope you will not fall into the hands of the British. If you do, you will be fighting with a rope around your neck."

10.
A Soldier Again

Pickens determined to fight, even if it meant he might be hanged. He would take that risk.

Once again he said goodbye to his family and rode over the neighboring countryside to recruit men from his old regiment. Knowing they would die by hanging if captured, some still chose to break their parole promise and join their former leader.

Together the militia traveled to General Daniel Morgan's camp on the Pacolet River. Pickens's group was small, but the men knew every path in the Up Country. Morgan, a Virginian, needed them to be the eyes and ears of his army in order to defeat British colonel Banastre Tarleton who chased him.

Without delay Morgan sent the militia to find out how far away Tarleton was, the size of his army, and the kind of artillery he was bringing.

The Wizard Owl organized his men and set out to gather intelligence. The very next day they returned with news.

Tarleton's troops, more than double the number of Morgan's, had crossed the Pacolet River and headed toward them. Thousands of green-coated dragoons with sabers swinging at their sides and red-coated infantrymen with bayonets were moving quickly. Worse, a three-pound cannon was being wheeled along with them.

Morgan directed Pickens to keep the information coming. Then he shouted commands to his men.

With wagons loaded, troops soon slogged along the muddy Green River Road to Cowpens, the chosen site for a face-off with Tarleton.

In the cold gray dawn of the following day, Pickens's scouts galloped into camp with news: "Tartleton is headed up Green River Road."

Morgan was ready with his battle plan. Pickens's militia, along with Howard's Continentals and William Washington's cavalry, got into position. They waited for the enemy to approach.

The green and red coats suddenly appeared through the trees. Tarleton's Redcoats and Dragoons formed a line to fight. When they began to advance, Pickens gave the order to his sharpshooters. **"Fire!"**

British soldiers were not backwoods hunters. They had not been trained to aim and fire like the

Patriots. Instead, the Redcoats shot from the hip. This way of shooting, without a true aim, often sent their fire above the heads of the Patriots. But the militia's musket balls rang true.

During a moment of panic, some of the militia tried to run from the British bayonets. Pickens headed them off, yelling above the blasting of musket fire, "Are you going to leave our mothers, sisters, sweethearts, and wives to such scoundrels?"

The call brought the men back to the battlefield.

Before long, the British soldiers had enough. Those still standing retreated. Tarleton managed to stay atop his horse and get away.

Though "Bloody Tarleton" escaped, the battle was a Patriot victory. A new wave of hope spread through the people of South Carolina. More important, the victory changed the way Congress looked at the South's part in the war.

11.
Making a Friend

There seemed to be no rest for Pickens and his men. Now, General Greene needed them to follow his troops into North Carolina and harass the British who trailed him.

In sleet and rain, the weary, hungry soldiers swooped down on the enemy. They scattered supply wagons and took food and supplies for the Patriots. Without heavy coats, they suffered from

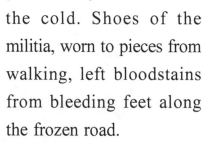

the cold. Shoes of the militia, worn to pieces from walking, left bloodstains from bleeding feet along the frozen road.

One morning Pickens saw a column of soldiers coming toward their camp. At the sight of a green jacket, he feared the British had discovered their hiding place. The green jacket, it turned out, belonged to General Richard Henry Lee, a Virginian known as "Light Horse Harry."

From the moment of Lee's salute to Pickens, the two became best friends.

In appearance they were nothing alike. Lee, dashing and bold, wore a flashy green jacket, white leather breeches, knee-high boots, and a helmet with a trailing white plume. Serious and conservative, Pickens dressed in a faded blue coat, worn breeches, and English boots with spurs.

Lee had come to join Pickens. That first evening the two generals made plans for their next move. Afterwards, they took cover from the cold under Pickens's blanket and went to sleep.

12.
Return to South Carolina

From January to March, Pickens and Lee supported Greene in North Carolina.

The Up Country militia had not one day's rest since they joined Daniel Morgan at Cowpens. The men had volunteered and ridden their own horses into the fight. They received no pay and no clothing. None even had an extra change of clothes. Yet they always did their duty without complaining.

Pickens knew they worried about their families just as he did. When he had an opportunity to do so, he spoke with General Greene on behalf of his militia. They wanted to go home, he said. There, they would be willing to take up the fight.

Greene understood and ordered them back to South Carolina. Their return to the colony, he believed, would "spirit up the Patriots" there.

Soon Pickens and his men turned their horses south.

When they reached the familiar Up Country, they faced what they feared most. Patriot homes stood plundered by Tories. Family members were angry and terrified, many packed and ready to move to a safer place until their men returned. The arrival of Pickens's militia proved to be a happy homecoming for all.

13.
A Heroine in the Family

As Greene predicted, the militia's return boosted the spirits of the Patriots. They felt safe again. Pickens's soldiers would not allow the Tories to get away with their old meanness. One Tory was heard to say, "Every bush has a Patriot behind it."

Most Tories feared Pickens and his men. Some even took refuge at the village of Ninety Six near the British-held Star Fort.

The King's loyal servants still caused trouble when they could. One day a small group of Tories rode along a dirt pathway through the Long Canes woods. Seeing a man on horseback he recognized,

one cried out, "Well, I'll be. Yonder rides Captain Joseph Pickens, Andrew's brother. I'm going to kill him."

A shot rang out from the Tory's rifle and Joseph fell to the ground. Ten days later Joseph died.

Sadness fell over the Pickens family. The general loved his brother. He depended on Joseph to help Becky and the children when he was away fighting. Now Joseph was gone.

The next time General Greene called for Pickens's support, the Wizard Owl did as many others. He took his family with him.

In camp, walking among his men, Pickens overheard a conversation. "The general's brought his family along," a soldier said, "but he's left ours behind to be butchered by that Tory Bill Cunningham."

Before going to bed that night, Pickens talked with Becky about her returning home with the children. She brushed her hair from her face and looked into her husband's eyes. She knew the pain he felt in making such a request. "I agree," she said. "That would be best."

Pickens called to his slave Pompey, who had followed him into war. Pompey would accompany Becky and the children home to the blockhouse and look after them.

When other wives saw the Pickenses' wagon packing to leave, one of them approached Becky. "Why are you leaving?" she asked.

Becky stroked the head of her crying child with a gentle hand. Lifting her chin high, she said, "Somebody needs to look after the plantation. If the women fail to do that, who will feed the army?"

Becky knew she must be brave, no matter how sad and scared she felt. Joseph was dead, and the enemy waited to kill her husband. Instead of crying, as she wanted to do, she squared her shoulders and looked in the direction of home.

14.
Eutaw Springs

Almost all the officers of the Revolution gathered for the Battle of Eutaw Springs. The night before the battle, two thousand Patriots lay on the ground just miles from Eutaw Springs. Their heads rested on exposed tree roots as they waited for dawn.

The officers' plan was to keep the large British force in the South occupied. That way, they could not head north to join Cornwallis in his fight with General George Washington. At Eutaw Springs, Pickens led the first line of soldiers into the attack.

During this battle, the bloodiest of the

Revolution, a rifle shot knocked Pickens from his horse. Believing him to be dead, his men carried his body behind the lines. To their amazement, they discovered the musket ball had hit the general's sword buckle. The force of the blow was so powerful, the metal buckle pierced his chest bone. The wound would give Pickens trouble as long as he lived.

The soldiers suffered injury too. With each firing of their muskets, the thick back ends, which rested against their shoulders, kicked. They padded their shoulders with folded rags and moss to soften the blows, but the repeated kick still caused pain and bruising.

Although the Patriots did not win the battle at Eutaw Springs, they accomplished their goal. They kept the British soldiers in the South from joining Cornwallis's army in the North. The British army was so weakened after this battle, they retreated to Charles Town.

About six weeks later, on October 19, 1781, the Revolutionary War ended. Cornwallis surrendered his army to General George Washington in Yorktown, Virginia.

Fighting continued in the South, however, for more than a year. The British still held Charles Town, and Tories continued to make trouble. Francis Marion and Thomas Sumter determined to fight until the enemy was driven from the city.

In December 1782 the British fleet sailed away at last from Charles Town. The ships carried not only the British army, but more than three thousand Tories and British citizens. Other passengers also shared this trip across the Atlantic Ocean: five thousand captured slaves.

15.
Final Cherokee Battle

The Cherokees promised Pickens they would no longer harm settlers. They also vowed not to take sides between the Tories and the Patriots. But, when Pickens left for Eutaw Springs, Tories talked the Indians into killing settlers in South Carolina and Georgia.

The governor of South Carolina pleaded with Pickens to do something about the rampage. Colonel Elijah Clarke agreed to help. The officers organized their men and marched together against the Cherokees.

The troops burned thirteen settlements in what is now Oconee and Pickens Counties. Then they crossed the Savannah River into Georgia to face Indian warriors there.

Each time the militia attacked a village, Pickens said to his men, "Our battle is with the warriors, not old men, women, or children. Spare them."

Finally, the Indians were ready to talk peace. "I realize," Pickens told the chiefs, "that white men have stirred up your people. If you will tell us who these men are, the war will stop."

The Indians gave up the Tory names. As always, Pickens kept his promise.

16.
Home Again

Pickens returned home to wrecked farm equipment and bare fields. On neighboring farms, only burned chimneys remained standing.

The Legislature offered loans to landowners whose homes and crops had been destroyed by Tories. Pickens used his money to rework the farm. He decided growing cotton would help more than any other product. It would supply clothes for his family, his slaves, and his neighbors.

The general loved walking through his fields, smelling the freshly plowed earth. As he directed the work of his slaves, the aching chest wound reminded him the Battle of Eutaw Springs was not that long ago.

Dick, always close by, scolded the general when he got his feet wet in the dewy fields. Pickens was grateful to this old slave for watching out for Becky and his children during his long absences from home. He made sure everyone treated Dick with great respect. As a small token of his own regard for the man, Pickens gave Dick a long knife in a leather sheath. Instruments of this type, which could be used as weapons, were not usually entrusted to slaves.

Since his boyhood, Pickens had longed for a home in the wilderness. As soon as he could afford to do so, he built a house on the bluffs above the Keowee River. He called it "Hopewell" after his church in Long Canes.

17.
Indian Treaties

When Cherokee Indians complained about whites settling on their land, Congress appointed Pickens to work with the Indians. Once again he put aside his personal duties for those of his country and joined other appointed commissioners to study the situation.

Pickens invited the Indians to Hopewell to talk. Chiefs and warriors came, dressed in leather breeches with a wampum fringe and wearing eagle feathers in their hair.

Chief Corn Tassel of Chota spoke for his people. "I hope we can live in peace," he said. "I consider you my brother." The chief recalled talks at Seneca when it was agreed the Cherokees would punish their own people for crimes committed, and the whites, theirs. "I am sorry to say," he concluded, "there are rogues among us on both sides."

War Woman spoke of peace and gave the commissioners a pipe as a symbol of peace.

The commissioners gave the Cherokees gifts of blankets, knives, tobacco, rifles, gunpowder, and tools.

Some of the Indians stayed on at Hopewell after the treaty talk. Pickens invited them for Christmas dinner.

Later, when Georgia began having trouble with the Creeks, George Washington asked for the commissioners' help. "Do what you did at the Hopewell treaty meeting," he told Pickens.

The commissioners met at Savannah, Georgia, and traveled down the coast to St. Mary's. There, a congregation of Creeks, Choctaws, and Chickasaws waited to greet them.

First, four hundred warriors performed an eagle dance in honor of the commissioners. In a special salute, they waved eagle tail feathers six times over the heads of the three white men. Afterward, they offered the peace pipe.

The commissioners listened as the Indians told them that whites from North Carolina, South Carolina, and Georgia were settling on their land between the Keowee and Tugaloo Rivers. The land was the home of their old town, they said.

"The settlers are not trying to take your land," Pickens assured them. "The problem is, no one knows the exact boundary lines between the colonies and your country. We are going to mark the lines so everyone will know. We want to be your friends and trade with you for the good of all."

The commissioners passed out many gifts, and both sides signed a treaty.

When George Washington received Pickens's report on the meeting, the president wrote to the general with a request: "If the treaty fails, I want you to command the fight against the Indians."

Pickens's letter in response was firm: "If the treaty should fail, I will help raise a militia. But I will not be in charge of it. It is too painful for me to fight against Indians who are my friends."

18.
Marking Boundaries

Several days after the meeting in Savannah, the commissioners, with the help of the Cherokees, began surveying and marking boundary lines between Indian land and the colonies.

The first day took them to Tamassee in South Carolina, land which is today in Oconee County. Pickens remembered his boyhood days at an uncle's home near where the Tamassee Indians lived. He loved that land between the fork of Tamassee Creek and Little River. He looked toward the mountains towering to the southwest, remembering. It was on this land he fought the

"Ring Fight" early in his military career.

The group often stopped at Indian villages for provisions before moving on. At night they made camp and hobbled their horses to graze. Through the Blue Ridge Mountains they followed trails so steep it took an hour to travel just three miles. In the valleys, dogwood blossoms colored the rich grassy meadows.

Finally, they reached Oconee Station, a fieldstone structure used as a military outpost. Rangers who would later guard the boundary lines stayed at Oconee Station.

The survey work took many weeks. Wherever the men found a place the horses could graze and have water, they threw themselves to the ground for rest. Travel was slow and the work of running the line hard. They covered hundreds of miles. Some trails took them through groves of sassafras trees. Others led them over jagged rock. Their movements slowed when they reached Turnback Point, a narrow pass in the rock. They continued on.

The men marked the boundary line by carving the year, 1797, into the bark of certain trees. On the north side of the chosen tree, they carved a "US" for United States. On the south side, a "C" stood for Cherokee Nation.

It took the group six months to mark South Carolina and North Carolina lines. Pickens reported to the Georgians that he could do no more. He needed to return home.

Benjamin Hawkes, chief Indian agent for the southern Indians, wrote the governor of Georgia:

> *In my opinion General Pickens stands higher in the estimation of the Indians than any man living. They have just cause to fear him as a warrior when he is their enemy and to love him as a friend and honest man.*

19.
Congressman

Pickens's stay at home did not last long. In 1794 he was elected in his district to represent South Carolina in Congress. South Carolina was ready to become a part of the United States of America.

More than anything, the general wanted to be at home with Becky. He longed to ride over his plantation and watch the waves of rich soil fall from the ox-drawn plows. He wanted to fill the barns of Hopewell with grain and breathe the scent of apple blossoms from his orchard. But the appointment was a great honor.

Pickens's family gathered to see him off to

Philadelphia. Becky must have felt proud as she watched her husband in his three-cornered hat, military coat, and ruffled shirt. As always, his hair, now gray, was pulled back in a queue. Pompey, Pickens's slave and companion in war, waited by the carriage, standing tall in his blue and scarlet uniform, to drive the old general.

Pickens handled his duties in Congress with the same determination and selflessness he used in his military career. He was not in favor of the country going into debt to form a navy. But he voted to establish a United States flag, to tax carriages, and to hire rangers to protect frontier settlers.

When Congress adjourned March 3, 1795, Pickens returned home.

20.
Last Years

Pickens settled down at last to the life of an ordinary citizen.

The area around Hopewell was now home to many residents. Because he had always loved the woods, he decided to build a home at the foothills of the Blue Ridge Mountains near Cherokee country and his Indian friends.

The area he chose was the site of an old Indian town. The Indians called it Tamassee, meaning "Sunlight of God." It was a place Pickens hoped he and Becky could live out their lives together. Their son Andrew, a lawyer, would move into Hopewell and run the farm.

Pickens stayed busy building at Tamassee and establishing a Presbyterian church as he did each time he moved to a new place.

When the wife of their son Ezekiel died, the Pickenses' two grandchildren came to live with them. Ezekiel was a lawyer and not able to care for the children full-time. The grandparents enjoyed having young people once again in their home. Pickens often talked to them about their responsibility as citizens.

Ezekiel's health failed and after a time of illness, he died. The Pickens had lost two children as infants, but this was the first of their grown children to die.

Becky tried to be cheerful through her grief. But she became frail and thin, and her own health failed. When she died, a sadness settled over Tamassee. Pickens rarely left home. He sometimes rode his horse to the courthouse when court was in session. And he liked being with old friends. He had given up his three-cornered hat for a broad-brimmed beaver one, and he moved about as solemn as ever. Everyone who saw him addressed him with respect.

When the weather was nice, he relaxed in the shade of a large cedar and read books ordered from Charleston and Philadelphia. He enjoyed letters from old friends and visits from his children and grandchildren.

On a warm day in August, at almost 78 years of age, Pickens finished his midday meal and gathered his mail. He sat outside facing the mountains he loved when he died.

A long funeral procession followed his simple casket over the winding road to the Presbyterian Stone Meeting House. In the cemetery near the site where the Indian treaties were signed, the Wizard Owl was laid to rest beside his wife Becky. His tombstone reads:

General Andrew Pickens
was born
13th September 1739
and died
11th August 1817
He was a Christian,
A Patriot and soldier.
His character and actions are
incorporated with the history of this country.
Filial affection and respect raise this
stone to his memory.

Pickens's will freed three of his older slaves, including Dick and Pompey. Each received land, animals, and farm equipment.

21.
Honors

Pickens received honors for the part he played in the Revolutionary War. After the Battle of Cowpens he was made brigadier general. Congress awarded him a sword, and the Senate presented him a gold medal.

During his lifetime he also served his country in other ways. He was a member of the First Constitutional Convention of the South Carolina Legislature and the first person from the Ninety Six District elected to the United States Congress.

Pickens is probably best known for his work with the Indians. Early on, he made treaties in an effort to stop war. Later, he served as a commissioner to see that Indians were treated fairly.

Many places, including the city and county of Pickens in South Carolina, bear his name.

The Indians called him Skyagunsta, Wizard Owl. To his fellow Presbyterians he was the Fighting Elder. No matter the name he was called, it was always spoken with respect.

COWPENS●

TAMASSEE●

Pae

Tyger R.

Enoree R.

HOPEWELL●

Savannah R.

Saluda R.

NINETY SIX ●

LONG CANES

KETTLE CREEK ●

AUGUSTA ●

GEORGIA

South
Carolina

WORDS NEEDED FOR UNDERSTANDING

about-face   a complete change of direction

acknowledge   show that someone or something is noticed

allegiance   loyalty

amazed   surprised; filled with admiration

artillery   rifles and cannons

bayonet   a steel blade attached to the muzzle of a rifle

bear arms against   fight against

blockhouse   in this time period, a strong wooden fort

bluffs   cliffs; steep river banks

breeches   pants that reach the knees

boulder   a large rock formation

canebrake	a thicket of canes, like bamboo
cavalry	combat troops mounted on horses
commissioner	a leader appointed to perform a certain task
compassion	feeling of sorrow for the suffering of others
conscience	a moral sense of right and wrong
conservative	opposed to great or sudden change; cautious
Continental	relating to a soldier of the American colonies during the Revolutionary War
culture	customs and civilization of a particular people
diverted	turned to go in a different direction
dragoons	heavily-armed soldiers who fought on horseback
dreaded	causing great fear

elder	an officer in an early Christian church
fieldstone	rough stones found in fields
filial	of or relating to a son or daughter
fleet	a number of warships together
frontier	the border between two countries with one yet to be settled
granite	a hard gray stone
Great Wagon Trail	a wagon road stretching from Philadelphia to the Carolinas, used by pioneer families traveling south from early 1700s to the Civil War
harass	annoy someone repeatedly
hobbled	in this case, tied horses' feet together to keep them from running away
huddled	crowded closely together
infantry	combat soldiers on foot

intelligence	information gathered for military purposes by spying on the enemy
justice of the peace	a nonprofessional judge
massacre	killing without mercy
meeting house	a building used for public meetings, especially for worship
mired	stuck in mud or soggy earth
military outpost	a place where a small group of soldiers is stationed, a long distance from the main army
militia	a volunteer group of soldiers, usually made up of ordinary citizens
moccasins	soft leather shoes
musket	a long-barreled rifle
occupants	persons who live in a home or place
outbuildings	buildings, such as sheds and barns, belonging to but separate from a house

panic	a sudden fear
Patriot	one who loves and supports his country; American colonist who fought for freedom
perished	died
parole	a word of honor promised in exchange for freedom
pitchfork	a farm tool; a long-handled fork used for pitching hay or straw
plume	a large, showy feather
plunder	take goods by force; destroy the property of others
powder horn	in this time period, the horn of an ox or cow used to carry gunpowder
powder magazine	a place to store ammunition
queue	a plait of hair worn hanging from the back of the head; a pigtail

rampage	violent behavior
ravage	do great damage to
rebels	persons who resist authority
recruit	enlist soldiers
refuge	a place to take shelter or protection from danger
regiment	a military unit
resounding	forceful
rogue	a bad guy; a dishonest person
saber	a heavy sword with a curved blade
scoundrel	a dishonest person
scout	a person sent out to gather information
scythe	a farm tool with a long curving blade attached at an angle to a long curved handle, used for cutting long grass or grain

sheath	a cover for a blade or tool
spring	a place where water comes up naturally from the ground; a natural fountain
spur	a U-shaped device with a toothed wheel that is worn on the heel of a boot
stern	strict; not cheerful
stockade	an enclosure like a fort, made of stakes driven into the ground
settlement	a community of settlers
surveyor	one who measures land
symbol	an object that stands for something invisible, like a pipe symbolizing peace
tomahawk	a lightweight ax, used as a tool or weapon by North American Indians
Tory	a person living in the colonies who gave allegiance to the King of England during the American Revolution

trading post	a store set up in the country where farmers, hunters, and tradesmen could buy and sell goods
traitor	a person who betrays his or her country
treaty	a formal agreement between two or more groups
trousers	pants
uprising	revolt against authorities
wampum	beads made from shells and strung together, used as decoration or money by North American Indians

THINGS TO DO AND THINK ABOUT

1. The name Long Canes came from the canes that made thick canebrakes in the bottomlands of that area. The settlement was close to the Indian trading path leading to the village of Keowee. Long Canes was located in present-day Abbeville County in South Carolina.

2. The word "Waxhaw" (used in the settlement called Waxhaws) comes from the Waxhaw Indians. It is said they took their name from the waxy-looking leaves of the hawthorn bush.

3. Unlike other Revolutionary War officers, Pickens did not feel the need to be "top man." Even after the Battle of Cowpens when he was promoted to brigadier general, he took orders from other generals when situations called for it. And always, he did whatever he was asked to do to the best of his ability. He was willing to cooperate with others to achieve a goal. What is your opinion of cooperation as an important character trait? Can you give an example?

4. Indian Chief Corn Tassel said, "There are many rogues (bad people) among the Indians and the whites." Do you think this is true today among all races of people? Can you cite an example where a

person or a few people gave a school, neighborhood, state, or even a country a bad reputation?

5. It is said that Pickens often talked to his grandchildren about their duties and responsibilities as citizens. What do you think he might have told them?

6. One of Pickens's neighbors said he rarely talked. "When he did," the neighbor said, "he took the words out of his mouth and examined each one between his fingers before he uttered it." Compare that to our modern-day expression "Think before you speak."

7. Did you know that the Cherokees, known as peaceful Indians, fought the Patriots because the British made promises to them if they would fight on the side of the King of England?

8. Did you know that the famous statesman John C. Calhoun was the nephew of Pickens's wife, Rebecca?

9. Did you know that Pickens was on the committee that made the decision to move the capital of South Carolina from Charles Town to Columbia?

10. It must have come as a surprise to Pickens's family when the watch Pickens sent to the wife of the dying British officer was returned to the Patriot general as a gift upon the death of the officer's wife.

11. After the Battle of Cowpens, Dick Pickens—slaves often took the last names of their masters—began to remove the boots of an officer he thought was dead. The officer revived to question the slave. When Dick told him his master needed shoes, the man acknowledged he was dying and did not need the boots. He did ask for a drink of water. Dick was happy to swap a drink of water for the boots.

12. Sometimes events in history can be confusing. This is true in the case of the "Ring Fight" mentioned in Chapter 3. A marker, erected by the Wizard of Tamassee Chapter of the Daughters of the American Revolution, stands near the Tamassee site where it is believed a ring fight took place. Several historians think Pickens participated in more than one ring fight since that method of attack was a favorite of the Indians. He won another similar fight, when Indians circled his militia, by having his men set fire to a canebrake. The fire caused the joints of the cane to explode. Indians thought the sounds came from gunfire and retreated.

13. It is difficult to trace all family members. Mention is made that Andrew and Becky named their tenth child Catherine after the grandmother who was killed by the Indians. Pickens's adult biography, *The Fighting Elder*, contains the names of seven children: Ezekiel,

Mary, Joseph, Andrew, Rebecca, Margaret, and Catherine. During that time period many babies died at birth. We know two Pickens children died, so there could have been others.

Historians disagree on the burning of Pickens's first home, which caused him to break his parole promise with the British. Some sources say Tories burned the outbuildings and crops; others include his home.

14. Pickens County Museum of Art and History is located at 307 Johnson Street in the town of Pickens. Among the displays are Andrew Pickens's dueling pistols and his walking-stick sword. There is also a copy of the Hopewell Treaty signed with the Indians at Pickens's home. A large collection of Indian artifacts are on display, as well as a collection of tools, including stone axes more than 6,000 years old.

Visiting hours are Tuesday 8:30AM–8:30PM, Wednesday–Friday 8:30AM–5:00PM, and Saturday 12:00–4:00PM. The museum is closed on Sunday and Monday. For information, visit the museum's Web site http://www.co.pickens.sc.us/Cultural_events.asp or call (864) 898-5963.

SOURCES USED

Babits, Lawrence E. *Cowpens Battlefield: A Walking Guide*. Johnson City, TN: The Overmountain Press, 1993.

Barefoot, Daniel W. *Touring South Carolina's Revolutionary War Sites*. Winston Salem, NC: John F. Blair Publisher, 1999.

Burgess, Mary Wyche. "Andrew Pickens: Treaty Makers Extraordinaire." Columbia, SC: *Sandlapper* Magazine, June 1973, 66-67.

Curtis, Judy. "The Bounty of Pickens." West Columbia, SC: *Living in South Carolina*, May 2000, 26-28.

Fleming, Thomas J. "Downright Fighting." *Official National Park Handbook*. National Park Service, 1988.

Hilborn, Nat and Sam Hilborn. *Battleground of Freedom*. Columbia, SC: Sandlapper Press, 1970.

Landrum, J. B. *Colonial and Revolutionary History of Upper South Carolina*. Spartanburg, SC: Reprint Company, 1962.

Roberts, Kenneth. *The Battle of Cowpens: The Great Morale Builder*. Mattituck, NY: American Reprint Company, 1976.

Waring, Alice Noble. *The Fighting Elder*. Columbia, SC: University of South Carolina Press, 1962.

Internet Site: http:www.nps.gov/cowp/pickens.htm

ABOUT THE AUTHOR

Idella Bodie was born in Ridge Spring, South Carolina. She received her degree in English from Columbia College and taught high school English and creative writing for thirty-one years.

Ms. Bodie's first book was published in 1971, and she has been writing books for young readers ever since. This is her twenty-first book.

Ms. Bodie lives in Aiken with her husband Jim. In her spare time, she enjoys reading, gardening, and traveling.

OTHER VOLUMES IN THIS SERIES

OTHER BOOKS BY IDELLA BODIE